T0157283

From Midnight till Dawn

TOM REED

WESTBOW
PRESS®
A DIVISION OF THOMAS NELSON
& ZONDERVAN

WestBow Press books may be ordered through booksellers or by contacting:

WestBow Press
A Division of Thomas Nelson
1663 Liberty Drive
Bloomington, IN 47403
www.westbowpress.com
1-(866) 928-1240

ISBN: 978-1-4908-0099-8 (sc)
ISBN: 978-1-4908-0100-1 (hc)
ISBN: 978-1-4908-0101-8 (e)

Library of Congress Control Number: 2013912284

Print information available on the last page.

WestBow Press rev. date: 7/25/2017

This book is dedicated with love to the late
Alice Elizabeth Saunders Reed,
a woman whose courage and smile endured many hardships
and also a woman who, by her life,
convinced me this book was possible.

Table of Contents

Acknowledgments

Most eminent thanks to God for His love, understanding, and patience with me. Thanks to Mrs. Evelyn Hollows, the mom of a neighborhood friend, the first person to take an interest in my poetry and encourage me to continue writing. Thanks to Evelyn Norris for her encouragement along the way. Thanks to Aunt Helen for her prayers and faith, to Aunt Dot for her enthusiasm, and to my dad, and two sisters, Wanda, and Debbie for their financial support and housing during lean times.

I will be forever grateful to Harry Connor for his warm and loving friendship and the countless hours (sometimes until midnight) he spent listening to and discussing my curious inquiries into the truth of the ages. And to his beloved wife, Libby, who with open arms and gracious hospitality opened their home to me and countless others.

Thanks to God the Father for giving me the gift of poetry.

To the Reader

From Midnight till Dawn is a collection of poems, thoughts, contemplations, and free verse portraying humanity's self-destructive flight through this realm we call reality. It is a device used to share with the reader my experiences, thoughts, senses, and spiritual psyche on my phenomenal journey in search of the truth. I also share with you some of the complex feelings I've experienced on this quest. The viewpoints reflected in some of the earlier poems do not necessarily reflect the maturity of my present viewpoints.

In 1970 I sat in a rocking chair on my front porch and wrote my first poem at the age of sixteen. The verses seemingly came out of the air, for I was not schooled in poetry in general or its mechanics. The name of that poem is "The Quest." That is when the journey began.

We must keep in mind that we are creatures of deeper substance than our immediate environment and that the universe is much larger than our earthly consciousness.

So turn the page and enter the journey.

Contemplations

Operator of life,
licensed by birth.
Destination bizarre,
escape from the earth.

The soul of creativity,
a never-ending trip.
What is concealed within the mouth
once you pass the lip?

Ever contrasting
and conflicting views of man,
curious but battling
the Master's plan.

A man must burst
out of his environment
before he can reach
his full potential.

It is extremely difficult
to be sane
in an insane world.

We should not become an image
in the reflection of life,
but strive to break the mirror.

One soul sings out
as a lonesome dove,
crying out for another soul
to comfort it.

We must recognize
the existence of our weaknesses
before we can become strong.

We must examine the negative
and harvest its positive potential.

Intelligence is
the amount of knowledge gained
but wisdom is
the application of it.

I returned
to the place of my childhood
and found decay.
I can never go back
only forward,
there are no endings,
only beginnings.

We must all
find the origin
of our existence.

All things
come from God
whether or not
they return to him.

A man is never alone
unless he is without God.

We must have faith
that anything can be accomplished,
or we have trouble
accomplishing anything at all.

We are in need of social reform
through the true word of God!

Anything without God is pointless.

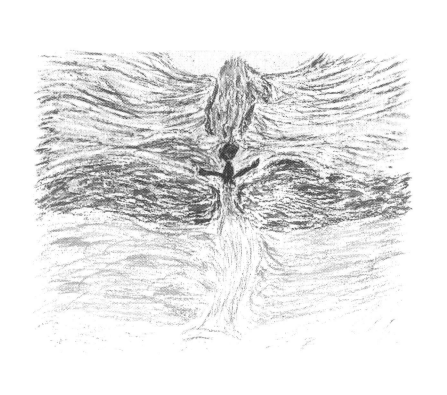

Evolution

From the sea it came,
with its singular cell?
Whether from heaven,
whether from hell?

Up from the darkness,
reaching for height,
with no destination,
just seeking new light.
Clueless creatures,
senseless yet fearless,
stumbling, fumbling,
reckless, and careless.

Multiplying fast,
capturing the land,
taking figures and forms,
dragging in sand.
Up from their knees
or down from the stars,
striving for freedom
while acquiring new scars.

Primitive skills
developed by time,
derived was a language
with reason and rhyme.

The earth was fertile
but altered by hand
by this new creature,
this species called man.
Envious greed
opened dangerous doors,
bursting forth ignorance
born into wars!

Through the land like a plague,
swiftly it swept.
The few who had noticed
silently wept.
Now marred in birth,
self-destruction as fate,
that distant-born creature
burst through the gate.
From the sea it came
with its singular cell.
Whether from heaven,
whether from hell.

Birth

When I first saw the light,

I cried.
Why?
Probably because it was blinding,
but I fought for breath to survive an unknown existence.

There were alien sounds,

voices beyond comprehension,
but how was I to know the constitution of sound?
Where I had been there was only silence,

wrapped in peaceful harmony.

Maybe it was instinct ...

when I cried.
A terrible feeling of desolation enveloped with fear,
for these beings, with one swift surgical move,

abducted me from ecstasy.

Exiled by birth,

I was banished forever.
Diffused, I was cold, hungry, and abandoned.
Each move I regressed, longing desperately for

my embryonic contentment ...
only to be denied ...

and propelled ...
into an existence even philosophers couldn't decipher.
So I lie in total abeyance ...

with time as my captor.

Plight of the Silent Star

The agony of self-destruction,
    caught lingering in despair.
People ponder in self-indulgence,
    never stopping once to care.
Listening has ceased to be utilized,
    and sight to near blindness,
presently presuming,
    never defying the depths with kindness.

Illusionary images travel
    past the brain's existence,
eluding the soul's curious grasp
    with strong, solid resistance.

Wings of speed captured by mortality
    has swiftly hasten flight.
Prisoners ramble, just a step behind,
    stumbling through the night.
Is there a doubt without recognition,
    a feeling not perceived?
Is wandering really homelessness,
    and the silent star deceived?

The tides of the sea rise and swell
    by the fullness of the moon.
What divine force combines the universe
    with mortal woman's womb?

A Poet Cries

Serenity in shades of green,
    filtering the sunshine through a prism,
    losing solace by the space of distance.
Springtime hues are oft inspiring,
    but the unfocused eye wanes wearily,
    falling ever deeper without entrance.

Cultivating barren wastelands
    and harvesting immortal suffrage,
    relics better lost than prostituting.
Champions gloriously bask
    in the coveted praise of pretension,
    while somewhere a lonely flute is singing.

Onward with foolish ignorance,
    the precious spoils going to the victor,
    the loser esteeming them more highly.
As the hounds chase with persistency,
    the fox gets fatter and lazier,
    evading entrapment, smiling slyly.

Harmony choking violently
    in a beginner's hands
    evolves into fluent finesse.
An artist in the pursuit of
    perfection leaves only
    distress:

    A beggar dreams,
    A legend dies,
    A flute sings,
    A poet cries.

The Quest

In the vast space of the universe,
multiplied by time,
I've searched the desolate planets,
even this earth of mine.
I have followed the ancient rainbow
to its very end,
finding an illusive dream
whose origin rests in sin.

When the snuffer of the candle
extinguishes the flame,
where is the guilty prisoner
in whom we place the blame?
When the souls of mortality
spring forth to rise again,
who will escape the price of hell,
and who will be condemned?

In the darkness of this dungeon
there shines a single ray
of our dreams, hopes, and fantasies,
clamoring for their say,
but distant wars of hatred
echo loudly in our minds,
and crimson red of reality
is all there is to find.

While trying to caress and calm
the angry, aging sea,
we do not wish to lose ourselves
in past hypocrisies.

Digesting Time

The storm was rabid,
tearing into the depth of night;
the mighty gales tossed my anchor toward the shore,
falling shorter than hoped.

Weariness comes from battles,
and sadness shadows the victor as well,
but the knight stands tall, never bending to the weight of despair
until alone.

Disguised as friend,
the vandal shrivels your body to wrinkles,
offering you treasures, but you ignorantly spent them on pleasures
that seem less than pleasing now.

So he plunders on,
taking everyone captive,
forcing submission upon even you;
no army is strong against a conqueror
who refuses to accept defeat as an answer.

And the masses follow
as they close their eyes and stumble through the darkness,
each step, deceitfully frivolous,
bringing them closer to finality.

Only the pursuit of truth remains:
Where is the unblemished face that saves
the drowning person in need?
In need of something more
than life____

Cocoon
(Twenty-First Birthday)

Wound tightly, layers and layers of decay,
twenty-one winters, the first as today.
Inside is singular, with never a crack,
falling helplessly through a world of black.

Trial

I sit upon winter's eve,
contemplating dark days to follow,
knowing no compromise with death!
A dagger, poised and gleaming,
prepared with full force to plunge downward,
denying me one last warm breath.

A victimless crime, you say,
where are your sense of morals, my friend?
For your eyes reflect my sadness.
Surely you must think it strange
dampness creeps within my very soul.
Do you think I'm lost in madness?

But enough—the hour is late,
the moon draped in an uncertain haze,
time a factor of survival.
Now I without amnesty,
left solely to combat the onslaught,
silent, I wait for arrival.

A hollow echo began,
softly at first but growing louder,
wisely playing time as a pawn.
Nervously I was pacing
back and forth, the clock ticking, ticking.
Beyond—the salvation of dawn.

Moments seemed like centuries,
stalling chances of deliverance.
An agonizing silence fell.
Again the eerie echo,
slightly faint yet astoundingly clear,
as if ascending from a well.
My senses, sharpened by fear,
following the movement of shadows,
I, concerned with the candle's dance.
For never was such a draft,
howling as if to beckon the dead,
still I cling to a single chance.

The core strength of sanity,
bizarre forces fight my secure mind.
I fought to regain my senses.
But tremendously louder
winds, like a sea of deafening noise,
weakening my defenses.

The locked window flew open,
giving entrance to the invaders
a hideous and ghostly sight.
Cold skeletons plundering
through dormant earth with deadly sickles,
forging a never-ending night.

Tension gave birth to pressure,
straining my sanity like a wire,
crushing my fortitude to dust.
Shrinking into the corner,
unbearable visions seized my brain,
buried under an icy crust.

Sanctuary in the fire,
betrayal of hope left no options,
my judgment bewildered by fate.
Suddenly I plunged forward,
falling short, my consciousness took leave.
Time lent no hand, nor did it wait.

Does your heart still have mercy
upon this vile, wretched criminal,
composed of such fiendish fiber?
To judge me sane or insane,
you must question your own sanity,
for I was a lone survivor—

Hiding

Indistinctive forms
camouflaged by shadows,
moving silently,
stealing silence from darkness.
Their only
witness is time,
bearing little relevance
to their existence.

Mystery lies in
their shadowy sanctuary;
they cry for salvation
from their darkened abyss.
Their eyes are narrowed
from the loss of light,
and their impoverished
minds feed solely on decay.

Where intruders are blind
they see with dimension,
but their vision
is gray, fading rapidly black.
If your vision's afar,
you mistake them as ghosts.
If you focus your eyes,
you may see them as self.

Mirrors

Once I observed a stranger
    confined within a glass.
As I moved, he moved the same,
    throughout a timeless pass.
I studied with intensity,
    curious to find
an answer to his origin,
    or futuristic sign.
His actions seemed so trivial,
    motives without sound.
When confronted with a question,
    seldom was he found.
His face was clearly visible,
    aging with concern.
Freedom was a two-way word
    that he had tried to learn.
He longed for the outer world
    with ultimate desire,
so I pounded on his prison
    with fists that never tire.
With accumulated strength
    that swelled from deep within,
I burst his cage with anger
    to find him caged again.

Naïveté

Lady Lost, I've stolen your eyes
    and heard your lies
    of unsung heroes.
To wager soul and sorely lose,
    captured in the blues
    of recent throes.

Frustration swells as abscess,
    releasing stress
    in deeds of balderdash.
To rely on dreams and newborn dawns
    and then find them gone,
    replaced by trash.

In land of yore, I played a king
    with diamond rings
    and castles tall.
But visions change from whence they came,
    dispelled by name
    in worried Mother's call.

Her mute smiling kept me fooled,
   and never schooled
   in what makes love from hearts.
When smile forced through pain
   on edge of life's terrain,
   'twas death or fresh new start?

Boy grew to man
   who couldn't take the world in hand
   or play their games of hate.
If searching for a pride-filled ego,
   I must say go,
   or woman wait.

For when you breach my eyes,
   finding my soul lies
   in yonder lands of wild.
Be gentle with good-byes,
   for the sadness in my eyes,
   is that of child.

The Song Is in Your Eyes

I've been to many places,
seen some empty faces,
even given my soul a time or two.
But all the songs I sing,
with all my soul can bring,
will be songs I sing to you.
I've never stopped to realize
the song is in your eyes.

I've tried my hardest,
and it's been difficult to find
the answers that I've searched for,
buried in my mind.
Your eyes showed me something
you've kept hidden from the world;
and we can lose ourselves in
love's own timeless swirls.

As the world goes rushing by,
poets never stop their cries;
lost between their lines we've failed to see.
We searched on earth and above,
looking for that perfect love;
let's begin together, you and me.
'Cause now I've stopped to realize
the song is in your eyes.

Yes, I've finally realized
the song is in your eyes

Perfect Pair

I think of you and remember
a full moon shining in splendor.
Rose wine was sweetest
I've ever tasted.
Your eyes sparkling with new light,
love was soft as the summer night.
Love I gave before you
seemingly wasted.

We came together so easy,
free as love we would share,
not even trying you pleased me,
we made the perfect pair.

I think of our love in motion,
a cloudless day in the ocean.
Drifting on rafts,
sunshine kissing our faces.
The cool summer rain would find us,
wrapped in a love that would save us.
I can't help but to savor
all the traces.

We came together so easy,
free as love we would share,
not even trying you pleased me,
we made the perfect pair.

Salvation's Empty Lady

Vast incomprehensible infinity,
    timeless, without leaving us behind.
Jumbled pieces with jagged edges,
    abstractions in the visions of my mind.

Empty corridors echo in silence
    replaced with faceless people in a crowd.
Ambivalence wraps me in her blanket,
    only to me the proud lady bowed.

Secrets of her soul she shared with me,
    betraying faith for passion for a while.
Why? I asked myself when she was leaving.
    To cease my soul she turned around and smiled.

Mirrors cast reality too painful,
    applauding surface figures seems so cruel.
Feelings of love obstructed by her hand,
    what lies behind the mask is a fool.

Soul

In the land of soul the light is warm,
the darkness cool with brilliance.
The soil is fertile, yielding fruits,
and flowers of radiant beauty.
Peace reigns o're and echoes love
from mount to deepest valley.
Truth and wisdom are pregnant seeds,
instilled in all men's minds.
Clouds are formed as face of God,
He guards our fragile hearts.
The shelter sought on earthly planes
is found within His realm.
Time is spent to beautify
the worlds which He created.
With the Master of Creativity,
I do dwell in soul.

The Last Poem

As circles break,
they form anew,
how swiftly they are gone.
Our love is where
we laid us down,
until the changing dawn.
I wish the sun
could let us see
as clearly as the moon;
But time has found
our dreams of love,
and timeless ends too soon.

Man slyly built
his world of greed
with lies he told himself.
All knowledge feeds
the hungry brain,
but wisdom yields to wealth.
The choice was made,
the die was cast,
the priceless pearl was sold.
How do you weigh
the loss of love
against a stone of gold?

I cannot change
the way you think,
and never shall I try.
So never shall
the dreamer speak.
He'll only make you cry!

Changes

The wars that scathe the human brain
are oft meticulous and maim.
Within the soul creative flair,
then steals away as never there,
returning
new another day.

Abandon life by taste alone.
Tis so difficult to condone.
The mastery of the art called choice
gradually starts to lose it's voice;
struggles first,
then softly gives way.

Just as crucial as birth to child,
to reap remains as one beguiled,
searching self in desperation,
losing sight of aspirations,
forfeiting
my illusive dreams.

In hooded shroud the specter came
and burst my world throughout in flames.
Minstrels sang melancholy songs
as hopelessly the world went on.
Tragic endings
till time redeems.

Dirge

We watched the heroes' fall
as we marched on through the night.
Stumbling ever onward,
further from the light.
The truth became so greyly vague
we couldn't realize
the inspiration leading us
was blinding us to lies, blinding us to lies.

A vision in the distance
beckoned us to come,
far away from violence
to a world where we'd be one.
Standing in freedom's doorway
a step ahead of time;
the shot that pierced that April morn
still echoes through our minds, echoes through our minds.

Power became the broker,
concealed within the cape,
one face to the nation
the other caught on tape.
Rumors spread like cancer.
Suspicions became true.
Stunned and disillusioned,
we can't believe in you, we can't believe in you.

Do we venture on from here?
The future's so obscure.
Marred in misty moors of doubt
still searching for the cure.
Wounded bleeding soldiers
driven to our knees;
the song goes on in sorrow
as we cry out to be free, as we cry out to be free.

Traveling Too Fast

Look in my driveway,
but no one comes to see.
Sit by my telephone,
but no one calls me.
Wonder if I mean
something to anyone,
life can get so lonely
after the setting sun.

People move so quickly,
swiftly they are gone,
in and out of love
before they complete the song.
I question where it leads
as the children grow,
a generation lost
what parents did not show.

Can it be we're traveling too fast?
Can't we stop and try to make it last.
Love as soft as candle's glow,
burning surely, burning slow,
is lost in darkness as these times.

Crowds passing on the street
blur into one face,
losing in a hopeless war
to hunger they can't trace.
Money cannot seem
to fill their empty holes.
They can't find a god
who can satisfy their souls.

Still greater darkness
has crept across the land,
shake my head in sorrow,
and try to understand.
No questions asked,
no one searching for the truth.
With the leaders lying,
the children stand aloof.

Can it be we're traveling too fast?
Can't we stop and try to make it last.
Love as soft as candle's glow,
burning surely, burning slow,
is lost in darkness as these times.

Age

Through a syndrome slowly dripping,
always dripping, never ending.
Time measures balance precisely,
forever stern, never bending.
Mere reflections never probing,
just consuming and condemning.
No compassion, strictly honest,
ironic jesters never winning.

Once is over, quickly passing;
climbing up is tumbling down.
What has been his will soon be ours,
never turning completely round.
Slow advances, second glances,
falling behind the trial we trod.
Mercy fails us; logic jails us,
wondering why, and where is God?

Life

As heroes fall one by one,
   no one's there to pick them up.
From seed to age superb wine
   pours sour in a paper cup.

Parasites that still remain
   cling out of desperation.
Ever-hungry souls of lust
   searching for incarnation.

While we barter for the ruins,
   ambition evolves to greed.
Tears are stained in crimson hues,
   as the fruit bears on the seed.

Journey Within

Spiraling downward into pitch-black hell,
    spiraling downward, rapidly I fell.
Ghost who haunt ghost doth inhabit such land,
    darkness unmatched harbor beast that eat man.
Grotesque and bizarre, perception supreme,
    distinguishes clear this land from a dream.
If this is life I am praying for death,
    if life after death, struggling for breath.
Limitless boundaries, infinitive plight,
    I must escape from these horrible sights.

Spiraling downward and inward for more,
    spiraling downward there must be a core.
Uniformed skeletons, soldiers of wars,
    aggressively charging, inflicting sores.
Rivers of blood flowing richly through towns
    where kings with their queens drank greedily down.
Gathered together, the vultures and hawks,
    preying profusely on forms that would talk.
So fear with its torture o're this land reign,
    piercing the mucus protecting the brain.

Spiraling downward into pitch-black hell,
    spiraling downward, rapidly I fell.

Escape

Dungeons of despondent dreams,
futile attempts of the mind;
Pressed within confining schemes,
assaulting the guts of time.
Scavenging blood of remains;
afflicting disease on self.
Emptiness within the frames,
filled with scraps of useless wealth.

Bursting with savage ruptures,
constantly craving rebirth.
Molded by deranged sculptors,
who created without mirth.
A narrow passage sighted,
bolting dash to free distress,
The inner eye is slighted,
sewn by a brilliant seamstress.

Armageddon

Four weeks the haunt has beckoned the mind,
familiar sights distorted by reality,
sunrise to set, to darkness, to where?
surprised by the looming length of finality.

Singular fuses into plural,
scratching the eyes of truth, distributing the shreds.
Seeping through cracks of passion are feelings,
lost within the boundaries of various beds.

Naked with the sincerity of Jesus,
then violated as rape to virgin.
Cleansing in another's newborn guilt,
ghostly figures of mysterious origins.

As the blood dripped from the eye of God
and wrath fallen prisoner to vengeance of wars,
weary soldiers face solemn defeat,
while I and the Devil battle in misty moors!!!

Thoughts on the Night of 10-19-76

This affliction goes beyond tolerance, and I was never one endowed with patience. When strenuous torment is compiled by the pressure of losing to the haste of time, the tendencies of insanity are enormously present. To comprehend sanity on this vast empty plane, one must rely on one's will of preservation.

Total devastation is a brilliant thought, but this action demolishes any prior efforts of sanity. As genius borders on the line of madness, the boundaries are indistinctively flexible.

Reality and fantasy are the most questionable opposites that exist. With a microscopic endeavor we shall examine the perplexity of their interfacial point. Reality is the physical space in which we occupy at the present measure of time. Fantasy is the transparent space the brain's thought illusions occupy at reality's present measure of time. The interfacial point becomes apparent when fantasy is transuding reality by physically acting out the fantasy our mind produces. The process transposing reality also produces reality.

Obliteration

At last the ruins have crumbled,
the fragile balance tilted.
Whatever hope remaining
was unraveled at the seams.
Harmony was torn to shreds,
by no means to be quilted.
Thirsty oceans feed no more,
Dusty are the arid streams.

The day turned night at noon,
without a star, without a moon.

Rebirth

Dim but visible,
recently dark but growing brighter.
Waking with tremendous energy,
vivid hues with new dimensions,
and sound,
whispers never heard before, amplified by listening.

Drained of the sickness,
hyped by seeing
sights of the freshness of a newborn child.
And dawn,
I've seen it now,
the night has lifted.

The rains that drenched the flowers were relinquished.
The golden sphere has chased the demons underground.

The stage was set,
the actor died,
performance of a miracle.

The Descent

There is a God, and He is just.
We mere men betray our trust.
From the garden sprang a foe,
when love carved clay fell into woe.

Eyes that once saw glorious light,
fell asleep into the night.
Awake yet dead in haunting dreams,
lost in time the conscience screams.

Can candle snuffed be lit as old?
Or doth sin besiege our souls?
And can we touch again the throne,
in whose image we were loaned?

The Answer

The answer lies within me not,
not even buried in my past.
The voice of prophecy is stilled,
off of life's vine the fruit is cast.
My quest was gold and precious jewels,
for kingdoms conquered at a glance;
For maidens pure and beautiful,
to laugh, to love, to sing and dance.
But the music echoed emptiness,
the lyrics without meaning;
And stones are cold as frozen love,
like the barren fields aft' gleaning.

Contemplating life's existence,
my passage through these mortal gates.
Philosophers expound with words,
the ear is full, my heart awaits.
The heart yearns with vivid passion,
amidst the turmoil, work, and strife.
The desire, the flesh, the bone, the breath,
seeks emergence from this life.
My spirit cries in anguished woe,
screaming into the blackened night,
"Which way to the immortal truth?
Where is the one eternal light?"

My heart desiring solitude,
was shattered by my searching soul.
Strange spirits came enticing me
to walk down ancient paths of gold.
Religions with a thousand tongues,
each with rituals to explore.
Seducing me to come with them,
fly back to time's beginning door.
"To what end," my heart resounded.
"is this surreal majestic dream?

And what tapestry of grandeur,
is sown with skill within the seams?"
Idols cannot speak with wisdom,
myths, shadowed by reality.
Legends' voices are quiet in death,
no hope in their finality.

Poised at the universal door,
I search for creativity.
Dark and futile ruins behind me,
infinity spans before me.
Tormented with despondency,
a desperate and final plea,
"Direct the compass free from time,
sail far away from painful seas."
Then came a light into the night,
and the darkness burst with seeing.
The spirit of eternal God
spoke into my earthly being.
A voice as pure as God's own Son,
His Spirit merging us to one.
I heard Him say, amidst man's strife,
"I am the Way,
the Truth,
the Life."

Destiny

The road that led us to these times
is the one that we must travel.
The strength of our God will endure
as His prophecies unravel.

The world is but a moment's pause,
the sighing of eternity.
The Master's plan is on the verge
of reaching its maturity.

My Statement to Mankind

There seem to come at this time an acquisition for my soul. A figurative triangle was drawn with Jesus on the right, the Devil on the left, and I, the dramatic point, was on the bottom with the past between me and the adjoining points. Now I was told it was time to dissolve the pyramid. My point of the triangle was aimed toward an uncertain future with no guide except my past.

Time has found me in an abandoned life.

The point at which I am is the fate of destiny. What is destiny? Is it a cataleptic state we inherit? Could it be we have no prior duty but to fulfill a purpose, and if we struggle against this purpose, are we void?

Facing infinity with a quarter of a century behind me, I am in suspension.

The rain is falling, but I am momentarily sheltered. I have known the cold drops of loneliness and the warm regeneration of love, but the desertion of both makes it hard to comprehend their meaning.

I have had love, and its radiance was beyond comparison. The space is still there untouched by time. What is that space? It is the loss of one's final commitment.

Loneliness is just a companion with deeper depths than ourselves, affecting our thoughts in depression with its omnipresence.

I have to stop and think. Why do I exist? Surely countless people have traveled these same roads.

I know the true meaning of life—to love others and be good to them. But I want to give them more than time. The world is such a contradiction to the meaning of life that true survival belongs to the few in numbers.

It is true that love is why God made man, but man cannot make His love, only abide in it. Why does man think he has the right to destroy His love?

Faith is a hollow word when trust has been abused, but we must look at the abuser to find the true meaning.

Hope is the light that darkness engulfs as it strains for a chance of existence. The continuity of hope and the strength of its existence enables hope to overcome the darkness.

Time has found me again. If we have infinite time, why does it always surpass us? Is it we must learn quickly so as not to lose to its haste? In learning quickly shouldn't we observe the present? Presence is the answer, is it not? We must have presence to exist, correct? So here I am at the present, considering the fallible future of my existence. What is existence? The state of being? The state of being what? What we chose or what has been chosen for us? Does anyone really know?

The situations in life are given to us for our benefits, but what are benefits if they are not used productively? Are they then to be like the wind that leaves us struggling for balance? Balance is a blessing that was given unto us and then mistakenly reprimanded by us as a child that was in the right.

Are souls to be bartered for? To be treated like a piece of land? Can we allow this bickering to continue, or do we have a choice? What are souls? In souls do we possess eternity? Are they our means for existence? Are they so important our ambitions are wrong? Do ambitions destroy what God has given us?

Time cannot be stopped, not even delayed. Can we? I believe we must take action before we destroy ourselves but in view of higher importance before we can find a way to destroy our souls.

I vote for God's plan. As Jesus said, "For this is the will of my Father, that everyone who beholds the Son and believes in Him, may have eternal life; and I myself will raise him up on the last day."

To The World

Because I am not
what you want me to be
you condemn me.
Because I do not walk
in the path of my father
or his fathers before him.

I should question your condemnation
but I understand.
You are of this world
I am not.
I have no home here
only passage.

I try to show you
a way to a higher existence
you cling to the old.
The old is destruction!
I wish not for your destruction,
rather for your salvation,
for you to experience
the highest transcendence
of Love that exist.

God knows the honesty
of my intentions upon this earth.
The grace of God is upon me
His Spirit flows through me.
For this
I am eternally grateful.

The truth is
I have departed from the world of man.
But man has also departed from my world.
A world where God
is the most important being;
where he speaks, teaches, and fulfills.

So
I do not walk alone.
If you see me walking
and I appear to be alone
speak to me for I wish to show you
the existence of God.

God
is the superior wisdom
that can save the world.
Or,
if the world will not listen,
at least you from the world.

Listen as Jesus beckons to your soul,
embrace him with your spirit
and receive into your depths his love.
Let your love become as his
approaching mankind with understanding
and compassion that breeds patience.

The teachings of the Master
are preparing us for a world
of total perfection.
A higher existence
surpassing any human conception
of Utopia.

God's hunger for our true love
inspired him to create within our souls
free will.
Within this power
lies the choice of eternal destiny.
To be an individual will away from God
and suffer death.
Or to be chastened by his will
and inherit life.

We are left
with opportunity and chance.
I do not believe in chance.
For God marries
opportunity and chance
with choice.

I bid you come
The wedding awaits.

The Touch

If I touch you
I touch you with beauty
With love that invites love.

If I stare into your eyes
I am searching for your soul
To unite with mine as one.

I don't mean to intimidate you
And in light shall I recognize you
Even if you abide in darkness.

With the same splendor of nature
We shall bathe in the regeneration
Of the Spirit that gives us life.

Then shall we fulfill the purpose
That was designed for mankind
Since the beginning of time.

We shall become
The children of God
And live in his love and beauty.

Serenity Falls

I sit and ponder as I stare
into the water's sunlit glare,
streaming through the trees above:
nature's grace and heaven's love.

Before I came I was ensnared
between life's endless toils and cares.
As the peaceful water sings,
solace to my heart it brings.

Where rocks and water meet the sod
is like the crystal eye of God.
Now my soul at rest can be,
and my dreams I truly see.

When noise and clamor doth abound
come sit awhile without a sound.
Spoken words impede the call
of the wisdom from the falls.

Creation

A brilliant light pierced the darkness,

                waters formed clouds and sea.
Gray-black rock amidst dirt and sand

                gave birth to grassy greens.

Ebbing and foaming, blue green seas

                crashing on pristine sands.
Dazzling crystals in the sun,

                no prints upon the lands.

Sun ruled the day with fiery sphere

                reflecting the moon at night.
Billions of diamonds splashed on black,

                earth bathed in silky light.

Sea was filled with swarming creatures,

                heavens gave flight to wings.
On earth roaming beast and cattle,

                creeping and crawling things.

Out of the dust filled with God's breath

                a living soul was made.
Out of his bones a woman's soul,

                the human race was laid.

Unfathomable paradise,

                mere mind cannot conceive.
Given with love by Eloyhiym,

                Creation's treasured seed.

The Sea

Waves rolling like thunder
onto the doorstop of my feet.
Sky married to water
with aroma salty and sweet.
Venturing past the roar
I now am drifting aimlessly
on gentle lapping swells
where ancient meets eternity.

A bed of greenish blue,
a canopy of blue and white,
I glance back to the shore,
then out to endless ocean's sight.
On land conflicts await
while peacefully I float along.
Sun warms my inner soul,
by Neptune's secrets I am drawn.

If I could choose my fate
and seal time's impetuous door,
I'd leave my life behind
drift out to sea forevermore.

Surviving

The shambles lie upon the ground
with naught a hand to mend.
The power gave extremely well,
but the players couldn't win.
The players lie and cheat to gain,
casting their every lot
What in the end to their dismay
will prove to matter not.
To share the blame, you share defeat,
for spirits never die.
Survival is a noble deed,
and strength will come from high.

Satan's Souls

Lusty souls, who are never quenched,
feed centuries on virgin meats.

Devouring hearts, destroying dreams,
enslaving lives beneath their feet.

Angry prisoners spewing hate,
wandering restless in this realm

to serve with fear and diligence
their evil master at the helm.

Aborted

Where are the cries
of the newborn babes?
Where do they lie
wrapped in warmth and love?

Silent heartbeats
in the moonless night
as God looks
tearfully from above.

The Light

If I seem bitter,
I am not,
only bitter toward the darkness,
for in the darkness are evil deeds.

The light is warm.
It is yours
to choose or deny in freedom,
the freedom darkness does not give.

Jesus

Jesus was a revolutionary,
a revolutionary with words and ideas from God.

A revolutionary armed with words and ideas
is more effective than one with sword and spear,
for those with swords and spears enslave the body,
but those with words and ideas conquer the heart.

Love

Love is the vitalization of being,
the simplicity of truth,
the bond of nature,
God's gift of virtue.

Love is greater, and goes beyond
the existence of life.

Time does not alter love!

Love is the spirit of the soul's ecstasy;
the power of the Creator's heart
on lesser ones.

Mortals Cry

Our passions thrown to summer's wind
will still be felt at Winter's end.
The rose so soft yet clutched so tight,
her fragrance yields not to the night.

Time spreads his wings and flies too fast,
fight as we may we cannot last.
The treasure that our hearts embrace
no mortal hand will ere erase.

With golden voices angels sing
about the jade and silver ring,
and as the stars fall from the sky,
for love misplaced the mortals cry.

Prejudice

Never seeing the light of day,
generations steeped in decay.
Why wander through this pointless maze,
blinded by the turbulent haze?

What is new about black or white?
But what God made in day and night.
Into one we should reconcile,
lest we travel our final mile.

Hate

Green with envy
Black with fear
Red with anger
Cold gray spear.

In View of Repentance

Through the ruins,
in this war of life,
I looked and saw
hope in His love.
Where destruction was,
God is now.
Where God is,
there am I also.

Beauty abounds
in His nature,
With love as the pulse
of His heart.
Truth is the
crystallization
to focus the
eye of the soul.

Why does man seek
to destroy life?
In His harmony
they could dwell.
Their feeble
efforts to create
has built their
world of illusions.

Will they never
follow His will?
Must the
prophecies devastate?
Please think
over alternatives
before the night
when time has flown.

Stagnation

The day has yielded,
    the night has fallen.
Time becomes stranded
    with no place to go.
A void has opened
    with cracks to crawl in,
covering the paths
    by the vines that grow.

Oppressing the murmurs,
    striving for sound,
is the force of night
    where silence abides.
Leary of darkness
    the light has not found,
but swept by a force
    compelling as tides.

A sleep as if dreaming
    falls like a spell,
losing control of
    what happens ahead.
From memory of old,
    a haunting tale,
in waking is lost
    in the morning bed.

Daylight streaming
    through the windows once more,
piercing the panes
    where no one sees out.
Consciousness covets
    a view through the door,
preparing the voice
    for one final shout.

Buried in the heart
    is news for the ear,
but out of its well
    the words must be drawn.
A rope that has stretched
    through many a year,
straining for freedom,
    now snaps and is gone.

Solitude

In the recess of
    my lonesome dwelling,
no explorers
    dare to venture.
Conquerors fall
    beneath the outer wall,
beat and broken
    with deadly wounds.

If only opened
    eyes would wonder here,
and steal my
    secret thoughts for use.
The prison would
    be bearable if found
before the stones
    are sealed with time.

Fatal Choice

What was once paradise
is now a battlefield.
Where once was harmony,
now men kill and are killed.

From the cradle of time,
still haunted by the choice,
never understanding
seduction of the voice.

Torn, beaten, and shattered,
earth rocking and reeling,
compass lost and broken,
only guides are feelings.

Right or wrong, good or bad,
the multitude decides,
while lurking in the wings
deception sways the tides.

Morals turned relative
confusing truth and lies.
Absolutes are buried
in the graves of the wise.

Ethics came to bow down
in front of politics.
Leaders became puppets
to power sucking ticks.

Ministers sold their God,
coffers overflowing;
while common men scrambled
for seeds worth the sowing.

Conflict ever-present,
our choice is day by day.
Earth is quickly fading,
and sky will melt away.

Who will live to record
the tale of all our woes.
As the sun yields to night,
we brace for final blows.

Prelude 08-17-82

I heard the voices sing of death.
I confess I will to follow.
For the world will fight the truest faith
and try to leave it hollow.

While I was thinking in a space,
where not many dare to venture.
No one doth call me now but death,
to depart a life that injures.

Allow myself a fleeting hope
to go against the tide again,
delay a fate life has preserved.
Which is the greater mortal sin?

Delivered through creation's door
to deal with earthly flesh and war.
Unto my soul the spirits come
and plunge their swords into my sores.

Death now singing its peaceful rest,
I listen with earnest yearning.
Yet in the quiet and feeble heart
there appears a greater burning.

A flame that stands amidst the winds,
like a fire upon the heavens
to reach a height above a world,
where there is no godly leaven.

Lord, have mercy upon the flesh
who searched in vain for flesh to join
and for the heart that no heart beats,
gird him with strength about the loins.

Please lift his feet and put them down,
always aligned with how you feel,
and guard him with the patience of
your steadfast, everlasting will.

The Prophet

The torture of a prophet's soul,
tears at his heart of reason;
on through ageless corridors,
the same through changing seasons.
His roots not of decaying earth,
but grown in a godly source.
People laugh and scorn his fate
and assail his peace with force.

A servant of God in honor,
but within man's eyes disgrace;
faced to roam forevermore,
he is exiled from his race.
Distant soil or familiar land,
his steps are ever haunted
by the darkness of men's souls
in bitterness is taunted.

O' Spirit of redeeming faith,
give your strength unto my soul,
let truth ring from muted lips
with the voices of the old;
the utterance of sacred word
upon world's forbidden ground.
Time has come to reveal him.
Now the prophet has been found.

Former Yugoslavia
(For Sanja)

Looking into your eyes,
I see a child,
innocent and running free,
dancing down the street
with flowers in hand
and hair blowing in the wind.

This was of course
before the war,
before they raped
your childhood.

Meaningless war,
long days, cold nights,
endless hunger of the soul.
When hope was lost
and heart was shattered,
desperation found you fleeing.

In your exile,
seeking refuge,
life is now
a constant struggle.

But sometimes,
looking into your eyes,
I see a child,
innocent and running free,
dancing down the street
with flowers in hand
and hair blowing in the wind.

Ancient Survivor

My life has been a collage of emotions,
    running like watercolors never focused,
spilling into a haunting portrait of intensity.

Once trapped by the hand of the Artist,
    the soul now yearns for freedom to join Him.

Time's prison is redundancy,
    and creative energy strains its boundaries.
Awaiting, the commitment has been made.

The paper, creased and wrinkled, lies still,
    with the heart of the artist still pounding.

911

Billows of smoke high in the air,
    ash and dust raining down.
Steel against steel burst into flames,
    spinning the world around.

Time held captive by screams of fear,
    chaos and disorder.
Spectators watched in disbelief,
    saneness crossed the border.

God of hate struck at god of greed,
    or so the thought had he,
while God of love waited with peace
    to see what choice would be.

Like the fortress towers falling,
    the wounded eagle fell,
and deep within the castle's wall
    struck fiery darts of hell.

Some brave soldiers gathered their strength,
    united as a ring,
and thwarted the plans of evil men
    to slay the country's king.

Guardians search the concrete tombs
    where fallen heroes lie.
Clinging on to desperate hope,
    grown men begin to cry.

Dark shadows fell upon the earth
    bringing the solemn night.
Democracy, theocracy,
    where is the dawn of light?

This day is penned on timeless scrolls
    for all to read and see,
the scars the eagle has endured
    in questing to be free.

New York

Bright endless yellow streams
    constantly in motion.
Pulsating rhythmic waves
    of a human ocean.
Concrete giants reach the sky
    with hawkers at their feet.
River joins the ancient sea
    where all the nations meet.
Far away from the roar
    of Wall Street's noisy crew,
twisting paths through lush lawns,
    Jacqueline's lake of blue.
Artist of ages past
    still live in hallowed halls,
outside artist struggle
    to hang upon her walls.
Phantom still haunts the streets
    that never see the night,
while Lady Liberty
    holds high the nation's light.

War

Spreading like darkness,
eating like cancer,
consuming the hearts of men.
Perverting desires,
corrupting morals,
where does depravity end?

Damaging psyche,
deluding the mind,
visions of glory and fame.
Demolishing bonds,
humanity breaks,
the earth is swallowed by flames.

Global Warming

Looming in the skies,
darkened with an ominous death,
a thinly spread veil,
thickened by greed, choking our breath.

Waveland
(Katrina's Aftermath)

Trees gnarled, bent and broken,
bowing down to the ocean's reign.
Mounds and mounds of debris,
lives of many therein contained.

Cars strewn like children's toys,
houses crushed by the angry sea.
Wood and stones lie in piles
where ghostly mausoleums be.

Beaten, battered, homeless,
people wandering through a maze,
seeking food and shelter,
caught stranded in a timeless haze.

Dawn brings uncertainty,
eyes of desperation pleading.
Who hears their hungry cries,
who will soothe their souls from bleeding?

Wide the heavens open,
an ear bends down to hear their prayers.
Love calling the hearts that beat for Him,
"Go show them that I care."

Death of Reason
(Death of a Nation)

The voice is silent. Without death,
the only sound is waning breath.
Time travels fast with single blink.
Pen is thirsty, devoid of ink.

Is there no muse in all the land,
inspiring thoughts to move the hand?
Where has the ageless wisdom gone?
Thrown to folly in newborn dawn.

Can we regain our sanity,
or yield to mental poverty?
Where will we go when going home
to Egypt, Greece, or mighty Rome?

Sailing on tempestuous seas
by winds of vain philosophies.
Protagoras, Nietzsche, Sigmund, Spock,
what hellish doors did they unlock?

But on with compass spinning 'round,
sailing away from distant sound
of wisest voice from which we hide,
Who placed the stars, to Him they guide.

To the President, Congress, and America

The trees are stripped.
They are bare.
Ground is frozen,
chill in air.
Winds of fortune
now are still.
Numbness shadows
what we feel.

We peer into
tomorrow
with nothing left
to borrow.
Disillusion
settles in.
Profit soars on
higher end!

Sold like slaves on
auction floor,
silent soldiers
back from war.
Disenchanting
mother's cry;
life is sold for
one more lie.

Does greed ever
drink its fill,
or shade with guilt
those who kill?
Has justice lost
all her sight,
Lady Liberty
her light?

There is greater
Light that shines,
shutting mouths of
roaring lions.
He will repay
when He comes,
all the deeds that
we have done.

Unless falling
on our knees,
with humble heart
make our pleas
to the God who
made us free;
which path holds
our destiny?

The Times

In the darkness I stumbled
My hand reaches to grasp the rope.
I miss and my hand dangles
Just below the object of hope.

Men shout loudly I listen
As their anger explodes the night.
I cannot but sometimes can
Understand their desperate plight.

Is the age of man a lie?
And truth captive by men of war.
Who closing their calloused hearts
They listen to the voice no more.

The enemy in plain view
Stands proudly speaking to the throng.
Comrade to this fallen world
Twisting right into what is wrong.

Sheep herds follow false shepherds
Not knowing to their destruction
Ignoring loving voices
Guiding paths to reconstruction.

So God waits with arms out wide.
Salvation calls the humble souls.
Love that understands the times
As now His ancient plan unfolds.

Beyond Gravity to Birth

Reaching past the dust of earth
Beyond gravity to birth.
Far beyond the starlit night
To the purest form of light.
Where no evil does dwell
Free from pain of human hell.
Promise of a sweet release
Ebbing tides of endless peace.
Love as pure as crystal streams
Fills full the heart as it dreams.
Angels singing with one voice
Praising Jesus for his choice.
Purging heaven by the cross
Redeeming souls, Satan's loss.
Hurled to earth Satan received
A kingdom here to deceive.
The world now in darkness fooled
By his tyranny are ruled.
Men professing to be free
Full of life and liberty,
Cannot see the chain that binds,
Self- proclaimed enlighten minds.
From a mountain truth does ring
With one voice the angels sing.
Reaching past the dust of earth
Beyond gravity to birth.

Depression

I stand in the midst
Of my fragmented memories.
With no congruent thoughts of logic.

A stranger stranded on a distant shore
Puzzled by this quandary of life.
Exiled from all rhyme and reason.
I am bereft.

Where is the vector of my soul?
As the full moon lights the night
But hides the northern star.

How much in darkness can one sink?
Until there is no day
And blindness obscures the path
Of light.

Dreams pounded by hail and freezing rain,
Driven by the harsh winds,
Into the frozen ground of earth.

Sanity pales into insignificance
Losing the restraint of
The disillusioned brain.
I am embattled.

The supply line was severed.
No route to escape.
Facing the enemy on his front lines.

Falling into the abyss
Of overwhelming despair
There is but one hope.
The Cross.

There on the blood stained wood
The steadfast love
Of the Lord never ceases.
There is salvation!

Prevailing Fate

The pain of life does not leave with a prayer or two.
Like a knife in the heart it twist and turns in you.
The wounded flesh cries and screams
the spirit stunned and dazed.
A fog descends upon the soul as a voice to God is raised.

Do you not see, do you not hear his sons and daughters wail.
The unjust deeds of wicked men seem likely to prevail.
Feet are shackled to the earth bound by chains with just one key.
Men complicate the simple cure the one device to make us free.

Standing in the ruins of life amidst the fallen world of man.
Born before creations birth the rebel to the Master's plan.
He cast his net to deceive he darkens human reason.
White against black, black against white,
Aleppo, Yemen, Ishmael's treason.

Now his face is turned to death to Jerusalem he slithers.
The fig tree sprouts prophetic leaves just before it withers.

Jerusalem

Jerusalem, my soul is crying for you.
The day is drawing closer than you know.
A man is rising out among the nations
to gather strength for one last fatal blow.

The Lord of Hosts had called you for His people,
His covenant fulfilled in Jesus Christ.
Your eyes were blinded by another vision.
Now He's reading you your final rites.

Jerusalem, lift your weary eyes.
Clouds of glory soon shall fill the skies.
The Spirit of the Lord is calling to thee.
Jerusalem, repent and be thou free.

In the midst of wars that rage around you,
in the face of constant misery,
can't you see your law was meant to guide you
till Jesus came to rescue you and me?

Jerusalem, lift your weary eyes.
Clouds of glory soon shall fill the skies.
The Spirit of the Lord is calling to thee.
Jerusalem, repent and be thou free.

Footnote

There is a somewhat bizarre but truthful footnote added to this manuscript.

As a child growing up in Sunday school, I was taught the usual Bible stories—Noah and the flood, Jonah and the whale, David and Goliath, and Jesus feeding the multitude. I don't remember getting into any detail about any parts of the Bible, and the portions that they taught us were very small. In 1979, months after the completion of the very first copyright of *From Midnight till Dawn*, I continued my ever-hungry search for the truth and began to read the Bible. I was concerned I might have missed the wisdom some said it possessed. I was extremely shocked!

A few verses from some of the poems in the earlier part of this book bear an amazing resemblance to some of the Scriptures I read in the Bible. In Matthew 24:29 Jesus says, "Immediately after the tribulation of those days shall the sun be darkened, and the moon shall not give her light, and the stars shall fall from heaven, and the powers of the heavens shall be shaken." The similarity of this Scripture and the last line in the poem "Obliteration," which says, "The day turned night at noon, without a star, without a moon," is just too uncanny to consider without wonderment.

In 1981 I discovered the poem "Journey Within" had three verses coinciding with the book of Revelation. "Journey Within" was written in the latter part of 1976. I had never read the book of Revelation before I had written this poem.

The verses are as follows:

"If this is life, praying for death,
if life after death, struggling for breath."

Compare this line with, "And in those days shall men seek death, and shall not find it; and shall desire to die, and death shall flee from them." (Revelation 9:6)

2. "Rivers of blood flowing through towns,
where Kings with their Queens drank greedily down."

Compare with "And the third angel poured out his vial upon the rivers and fountains of water; and they became blood. And I heard the angel of the waters say, Thou art righteous, O Lord, which art, and wast, and shalt be, because thou hast judged thus. For they have shed the blood of saints and prophets, and thou hast given them blood to drink; for they are worthy." (Revelation 16:4-6)

3. "Birds were but crows, vultures and hawks,
    preying profusely on forms that would talk."

Compare to, "And I saw an angel standing in the sun; and he cried with a loud voice, saying to all the fowls that fly in the midst of heaven, Come and gather yourselves together unto the supper of the great God; That ye may eat the flesh of kings, and the flesh of captains, and the flesh of mighty men, and the flesh of horses, and of them that sit on them, and the flesh of all men, both free and bond, both small and great." (Revelation 19:17-18)

In the 2002 revision I did not change the meaning of any of these lines, and I did not adapt or manipulate any of the words to try to say anything that was not there to begin with. I only revised these poems for better cadence and meter.

I have no remembrance of reading or knowing these Scriptures before I wrote these poems.

No one knows the day or hour when Jesus will come back. Only the Father who is in heaven knows that, but we do know He will come back. He will fulfill His promise and God's Word to us. I believe the poems "Obliteration" and "Journey Within" are a witness to this fact. I did not receive Jesus Christ as my Lord and Savior until November 1979 when I was twenty-five. Both of these poems were written and copyrighted before that time.

My aim is not deception but the truth. The truth has prevailed in these works, but the final choice is yours—to believe or deny. Please consider this seriously!

Sincerely,
Tom Reed

About the Author

I believe God gave me the gift to write poetry. The book is about my life and events happening in the world during my lifetime.

I started writing poetry when I was sixteen and had an unquenchable thirst for the truth. I was curious and always wanted to know what the reality was behind the illusions of life. I searched, finding mainly despair, disillusionment, and futility, sometimes to a suicidal point. At twenty-five I was at the brink of hopelessness, and I read where Jesus said, "I am the way, the truth, and the life." A light flooded the inside of me, and I knew I had found the truth. I received Jesus as my savior, and my life has been changed ever since that moment.

Printed in the United States
By Bookmasters